Dedication

This book is dedicated to my God, husband, daughters, parents, brothers, sisters and great friends! Also, with great gratitude, I want to thank bad bosses, crappy coworkers, back stabbers, heart breakers and haters for motivating me to be and do more! Because there is no glory or testimony without challenges or controversy!

Chapters

Family *(A group of persons related by descent or marriage)*................1

Friends *(A person whom one knows, likes, and trusts)* 10

Focus *(To have clarity, as of attention or activity to concentrate)* 13

Fear *(A very disturbing feeling, uneasy and apprehensive about danger)* 15

Finance *(The management of money, investments and credit)*. 18

Freaking *(Sex and Dating)*. ………………….……....….…..23

Fitness *(The condition of good health, exercise and proper nutrition)*. 28

Frustration *(A feeling of dissatisfaction, anger, anxiety or depression)* ..31

Faith *(A belief or teachings of religion)*. ……………....…………...35

Finally *(Your legacy, what will people say about you)*. ………..……38

What the F is a book I had wanted to write for some time! I came up with the title after watching a news story about a critically ill father who had written a book for his daughters. I thought to myself what an awesome idea because tomorrow it is not promised to anyone. I sat and wondered within me what life lessons would I had preferred to have known more about before I learned things the hard way. I understand that trials and tribulations help you to grow as a person and mature, but there are some things I just didn't want my daughters to go through in life if I could help it. So, I started to brainstorm on a few topics and the first was finances, second friendships and then faith. As I continued to make my list, I realized I had a pattern and that was the letter F. For some reasons, it was constant and so I knew I needed to use it in my title. I actually thought of calling my book F stands for or Lessons in F and many other F ideas, but What the F was bold, and it caused curiosity. I figured out that others would want to know What the F I was talking about. I was two weeks shy of turning 41 when I decided to write my book and gave myself a year to get it finished. I knew that finding the time would be hard and going over every thought about each subject could possibly cause me some depression. So, I decided to find other women to work with me. I figured out the different experience and thoughts made for a better connection with reader's and a diversity of outcomes and lessons. I wanted women of all races, ages and I asked that they only picked one topic and give their first name and age. Some wondered why I wanted just a first name, and this was to give the story's creator some deserved credit but at the same time obscure. I believe that age has a lot to do with how we react to situations and challenges, and so I felt it was important to add the age to the creator's lesson, so that readers could connect even better. In this book, you will read about my experiences and opinion about everyday topics. At times, you might find some of the stories sad, but don't be surprised if you find yourself laughing out loud as well. After all, how fun would life be without the roller-coaster of emotions and experiences? My hope for all who decide to take a glance or read this as an opportunity to learn from others, a greater understanding of self and a realization that you are not alone in this battle we call life. So, with that, What the F let's start reading!

Chapter 1:
Family

I'm starting this book with family as my first chapter because these are the first people you will interact with, and the first set of individuals to challenge you as a person. These are the people who will build you up, break you down, and teach you the ways to move and how to brush off disappointment when things don't go your way. Now, at some point you will be placed in almost every role a family should offer. So far, I have been the mean older sister, the go to daughter, teach you a lesson mom, penny counting wife, ambitious granddaughter and hopefully one day sweet grandmother. However, I always try to put in my best into every role even the one's I feel that does not really represent me. Like everybody else, I also found myself in a state of wanting to say, "I don't give a damn anymore," drive off and maybe find a new family. But since I'm afraid of driving pass 65 mph and can't cope with the stress of the highways, I have been forced to settle with the family I was naturally born into, Yay lucky me! Now, I would like to think I have always been this awesome creative woman who is waiting to brighten up the world, but the truth is that my parents and siblings have had a major influence on me. Each year at home, I had plenty of experiences that molded this sensitive, creative and intense alpha personality that you are seeing today.

I am the oldest of six children, and my first role was being a daughter and catering for my siblings. I was born to a teenage mother who was 16 at the time, and my father was 9 years older than her and a man who lived his life on the streets. My mother was very affectionate, fun but tough and I admired the kind of love she always showed us. She kisses us goodnight and always said "I love you" to us before going to bed or leaving the home. My mom was a pretty easy-going woman if you did alright in school, told the truth, did your chores regularly, were dependable and graduated on time you were going to be alright with her. My father has always been very tough, and in every way, I would describe him as a hard man who believed in a universal language and tough love. Now I know you're thinking to yourself what is universal language all about? Well that means that you talk equally to everyone without any form of sentiment attached. It doesn't matter if you are old, young, my kid or even a stranger, everybody is getting the same treatment. So, if you spill Kool-Aid on the carpet or if you are a random man who just told my dad to shut up, the outcome was most likely going to be the same. So, I often found myself crying while talking to him, but strangely admiring his I don't give a damn about everybody attitude.

I really wanted to be my father's precious flower, but gentleness didn't make me the strong outspoken woman I am today. I also had a stepfather who married my mother when I was very young. Their relationship was strained and uncomfortable for me. He was a military man from the south. So, at times it felt like I was in boot camp with a fast-talking drill Sgt. who looked at you in ways that you just couldn't read and understand. As a child, I loved my real father even though I knew he had serious problems with my mom. After all, he was my father and what girl doesn't love her daddy. When I was younger, my parents didn't push us to high educational expectations and being at least average kept me out of trouble. Please, don't get it confused trying to maintain a C or C- was hard work as well especially, when you don't study. First, you must master turning in all the class work because you can't pass the test when you don't study or your 2nd option will be to study some for the test and get at least a 70 because you're missing class work. However, getting a "C" on my report card was like an A to me because I worked hard for it and to be honest, I should have received at least fifty cents for each C I made instead of my mom saying, "You can do better and you better be glad there isn't any D's or F's on here." I was always in trouble for talking in class, in fact, I believe my report card always said "Talks excessively in class" from Pre-K to 10th grade. I just really enjoyed learning about people and what they did when they got home. I wanted to know what they ate for dinner, who they talked to on the phone and if the porn came through on their TV every three minutes. Back in the day you could get clear pictures on the screen every few minutes on pay per view. At that age, I was fascinated with the idea of sex. However, ask me how to spell caring in the 6th grade and I probably would have spelled it as K.E.R.N.I.N.G because that's how it sounded, and studying was out the picture. My behavior almost had my butt back in the 6th grade because I didn't take my mother seriously. All it took was a beat down and a promise to be back in 6th grade at the same school to fix that problem though. My parents taught me early that my actions had consequences and I will be honest with you; I was afraid to disobey their rules. Every time I tried to feel myself, I was brought back to reality. As a kid, I just looked at the rules and chores as a form of child slavery. I really felt like Kunta "Scott" Kenta. All I heard was do this, do that, get me this, why did you do this and why didn't you do that! I couldn't wait to grow up and do my own thing and live life the way I wanted. Sounds familiar to anyone? Since my parents set the foundation of discipline, I eventually learned to just say 'yes ma'am' and never stare at my mom when she was yelling at me and I could live to talk about how crazy she is the next day to my friends. By the time, I reached 14, I had started working and taking an intense liking for the boys! The job was a plus because it gave me something to look forward to and I didn't have to beg for a dollar here and there. The boy thing was different because even though I thought I was hot stuff, most of the boys didn't give me any attention. I was skinny with a big forehead, short hair, acne and small boobs. I was rocking a little junk back then but Jenny from the block had not made it cool yet. Understanding that my parents needed to trust me and knowing I was not just responsible for myself but also my siblings, made me grow up fast, to shoulder so many responsibilities. Showing I could be reliable and independent allowed my mother and I to have a great relationship for some time. I could talk to my mother about anything because she was not just my mom but my best friend. She trusted my decisions because she knew I would do my best to keep my word or talk about any issues with her if I was struggling with something. My father and I were always at odds. He was a very head strong man, but for reasons you wouldn't expect. I was always looking for his love and he was always too stubborn to give it. I spent most of my childhood wishing I could be the apple of his eye, and I longed to hear him say he was happy I was his daughter, but many times I heard the opposite. The amazing thing I finally came to realize, once I hit 40 about my relationship with my father, was how strong I was and how that relationship allowed me to stand, when I had no one to lean on. It allowed me to enter a room full of people who didn't care for me, it allowed me to be my own person instead of following the crowd, and it gave me a false sense that I didn't need validation, when I sometimes wanted it. I was tough, I was a leader and I played to my own tune because I didn't need anyone to tell me who I am. This skill gave me the strength to leave home after high school and to take on many challenges throughout my life. My childhood wasn't great, but it had moments when I knew love. I felt it in my mother's hugs, my sibling's laughter and the encouraging words from friends and teachers. So, I try to live my life remembering the good times to deal with heartaches and disappointments of my childhood. No family is complete without the older smarter sibling! These wonderful human beings are the Kings and Queens of the family. They have a court of the usual suspects like: The Court Maids, better known as the sibling that does things for you, that you both know they shouldn't. The Confessor, better known as the snitch sibling. The Royal Fool, better known as the comedian of the siblings who is always out for a laugh and The Knight, who is willing to throw down at any time, with anyone who says something about them or their momma. The oldest is The Teacher of taunting, hidden punches, style and what not to do. They are the ones who get to talk crap about you and start a fight with someone else who keeps it going when you start to cry. I loved playing tricks on my siblings and it was real fun. They eventually tried to gang up on me but by the time they were old enough, I had become a master at it. As the oldest of six children, I had the great pleasure of being my parents test dummy. Yes, so I got the worst beatings, the best presents, the most love and no handy downs. I also got to be the third parent responsible for cooking, cleaning, getting others ready and watching the kids every time we left our house because nobody got time for that! As the oldest, you will set the standards for your siblings and they will either want to be like you or try their hardest to be the opposite. The verdict is still out for me. I didn't necessary feel like a leader, but I took my role to look out for my siblings very seriously. I tried my best to be their big sister even when they grew up instead of just watching from the side line and waiting for them to ask for help. This allowed for some conflict, but eventually I learned to step back a little bit! As the oldest, I always see myself as the protector and head lion of the pack no matter how old my siblings were. I will always give of myself when I don't want too, and I will always find myself thinking of them even when feel they don't care about me. My sisters and brothers mean the world to me because they were my first friends, enemies and collaborators of shade. I greatly appreciate having such a diverse and talented group to call my siblings. They taught me how to hold my own in verbal judo with any man or woman who decided to tango with the Queen. As a girl, I just assumed I would have a rich husband someday. I would also have all the material things rich people had; a big house, fancy cars, vacation homes, travel and a plastic surgeon to keep me tight and fine. I figured that people grew up poor and then turned rich, and rich kids would grow up and lose everything. I wasn't Annie, but my future husband would be called Mr. More bucks. I wouldn't work but just volunteer my time and create art in my studio. People would talk about how great we were together and ask the secret to true love. My two kids, a boy and a girl, of course would be well mannered, smart, talented and of course beautiful. Yes, the best fairytale written if I say so myself, but of course, I can't live on the pages of a book and like many others, life isn't easy, and I was no exception to the rule. Let's just say getting a ring on it was harder than I thought, and even after all the struggles, it's still required hard work.

Being in a relationship is a mix of creativity, loss, awareness, jealousy, self-doubt, pride, joy and pain, which some call the roller-coaster of love. Let me tell you, this ride doesn't stop because you got a good job, won an award, saved a few lives, lost ten pounds or got married; in fact, it becomes more intensified. I have been married for 17 years and it's been some long, long, years! However, more often I realize that there is no other place I rather be than next to my husband on the couch watching TV. I still don't know him 100 percent because we continued to evolve as we get older. Being a wife is awesome to me, but marriage is not an easy situation for two people to be in. I am an advocate and user of couple's counseling because sometimes I need to learn to hear and listen openly and honestly about my husband and my own needs. We are often so fast to point out other people's flaws and blame someone else for their mistakes. Like anything else, if you really want it you should work hard to get it and maintain it. But the hardest job in the family is that of a parent. So, I have two children just like I predicted but God didn't see a son in my fairy tale. They are my pride and joy. They have the perfect mesh of myself and my husband, with their looks and personalities that keeps us busy, even in our sleep. I thought the love I found in my husband would be the greatest love I could know until I had children. I swear as hard as I try to be stern and orderly, they have a way of melting my heart just a little. As a mother, I worry about them meeting a man who will someday make them cry, a friend who will betray their trust, a devil who will try to steal their joy and all the other ways this world makes us feel unsure of ourselves. I want to protect them, but I know I can only do so much but prepare them for what I know and hope they have the strength to deal with what is new. I find great strength in the smiles and hugs of my children which are needed often to light up my day. I pray that my words don't leave a sour feeling inside when they think of me and that they understand I love them more than myself. I hate knowing that my ideas will someday become old school and sitting in the bathroom just to chill while I poop will one day go away. I pray that I raise strong women who love their children as much as I do. I am forever grateful that I was given the opportunity and responsibility to mold two lives. It has been the most challenging and rewarding goal of my life. I have a lot of cousins and I mean a lot of cousins! My father is 1 of 12 kids and my mother is 1of 5. I've had no relationship with most of my relatives due to being raised out of the country, but mainly we just weren't close. I have family all around the United States and found out about a year ago, that a boy I crushed on for years and finally got to date was like a 5th cousin. Thank goodness, I was physically not able to give him any cookies, because he could have been my baby daddy. I do have a few cousins, aunts and uncles who have been active in my life at some way or another. I really enjoy being around family, when we are not fighting or talking about each other. I have even looked to a few members of my extended family as my style and career leaders. I used to think if I could have my Mother's looks, my stylish 2nd Cousin's fashion sense and my Aunt's big gold tooth smile and economic status. They all made me see myself as a success and without role models, how do you know where you want to be or how to get there? I have some of the funniest, realist, non-judgmental and caring people I have ever known in my family. I am forever grateful to those who have added to my self-esteem and self-worth, and I hope that one day I can do the same for a family member. However, I also have had some negative members who would often sit in a sinking ship and I would acknowledge them with a prayer and keep on peddling on my way. Our family can't be picked out for us, we were just born into the storm and then try to live through it. Most of us will carry scars from some traumatic events, but if we take the time to look at our life and events with our family, we will find a lot of good times and lessons that will make us better people if we take note.

Chapter 2:
Friends

I have always been the type of person who likes to talk and meet new people. I am also the type of person who must be convinced to follow others as well. I have always been a strong-minded person, and this has been a blessing and a curse when it comes to making new friends. When I was younger, I wanted to fit in and be popular, but I didn't have the looks, cloths or personality to make everyone's friend list. I was never a bully and sure in hell didn't let anybody bully, me even if it meant me coming home dusty with holes and my hair looking like 14 monkeys styled it! I guess my personality was a combination of nature and not having anybody to have my back. I won't say I didn't have my moments of wishing for more friends or feeling jealous of those who were popular, because I really did. Being a military brat allowed me the chance to be around all races at an early age, so I never paid real attention to these differences when I looked for friends. But once I came home to Portland Oregon, I learned quickly that others saw a difference. I remember being in third grade and being called the N word during lunch time and having bark dust thrown at me, which wasn't really cool at all. I was the only African American in my class. Even though I was fair skinned, it didn't keep me away from the name I was called by the other students. I learned I was different and would either let it hold me down or let it make me stronger. I was the oldest, so I had to pick the leadership role, because I refused to let my siblings, see me as anything other than a leader. Besides, it's hard to tell your siblings what to do when other kids can make you cry. In Elementary, Middle and High School, I had a few fights, but one of my best friends to this day came from a fight. In fact, it was over a seat that didn't belong to either her or me in 6th grade. I share that to say fighting doesn't always lead to continuous aggressive behavior, sometimes it helps you make friends. I was trying to play a prank (told a boy in our class how she wanted to date him and talked about him all the time) on another close friend when we started our lifelong friendship. I have always been a person to have only a handful of friends and a dozen associates. I personally think it's because I'm so transparent, honest and animated. I'm not the type that will lie to you or be on your side when you're wrong, but you will see me cheering you on and supporting you all the way through whatever goal you are trying to achieve. I am your number one fan because I love seeing my peeps excel and do great things. I truly believe that if I have surrounded myself with smart, beautiful, motivated, honest and loving friends the better person I became. I enjoy learning about life and learning more about myself. Most of what I have accomplished in my life has come from watching others accomplish things I had made excuses about. If you are someone I call a friend, just know that I value your opinion and you mean a lot to me. I look up to you in a way you will not understand, and I admire your personality. I believe Drake said it best "I got fake people showing fake love to me straight up to my face". Oh, man have I been the victim of this many times in my life. To be honest, I am not sure why! I'm average in looks, money, and style. I am also cheaper than

Julius Rock from 'Everybody hates Chris.' I'm funny, outspoken, dependable, organized and I don't talk behind your back. I also don't borrow money, ask to use your car, sleep with your man or come to your party without bringing anything. I have been blessed to see over time who my real friends are, and even though they are far away, I know that any time I need their advice or support, they will do all they can to be there for me. No matter how long we are apart, our conversations don't skip a beat. In a nut shell, finding real friends can be extremely difficult. Keeping friends can be just as bad but when you have a friend, a real friend doesn't take it for granted, and just like any good relationship, it takes communication and compromise.

Chapter 3:
Focus

Having the determination to do something and see it through can be very difficult when you have a mind that runs a thousand miles in a minute. I swear the right side of my brain has taken over the left because I can't sleep without dreaming, but I can pat my head and rub my tummy. This too can be very difficult for those who lack creativity and coordination. Anyway, if I could make money from the ideas that cross my mind, I wouldn't be so stressed about keeping a job. In the last eleven years, I have held four business licenses and none of my so-called ideas have made me more than $217. Each license cost $75, and so I really lost $85 with my ideas. The reason I didn't succeed wasn't because my ideas weren't good, but because I didn't focus enough on one task to make it a success. I would start off all excited and two months in, I would be hit with life or a new idea that would then take on all my free time. This was the same reason I owned about 40 wigs. I can't commit to a hair style or color for more than 7 days before I get bored. I have wanted to be a police officer, interior designer, choreographer, reporter, author, actress, mascot, house flipper, day care provider, teacher, counselor, preacher, talk show host, makeup artist, soup cook, stylist, personal assistant and recently, a video vixen but at 41 with some extra handles, I don't see that working out. I can remember a few times I have been focused and diligent to accomplish things. The first time was in 6th grade, when I was threatened by my mother to repeat the 6th grade, at the same school. I had used all my class time to talk and get to know my classmates and it reflected in my grades, which I hid from her most of the year. One day, when the progress reports I had failed to retrieve made it to my mother's hand and resurfaced in a long ass whooping along with this threat, I learned I could be focused and turn the D and F's into C's with lots of begging to my teachers for help and extra credit. The next year, I wanted to win a talent show, and in the spirit of Joe Jackson, I made my siblings practice repeatedly with me until we had it. Of course, we won whatever it was and had a lifelong memory of its experience with a video to show every few years to keep us embarrassed. These accomplishments, yet small were the beginnings of making my dreams into reality. If I build it, maybe they will come but if not, at least I can say I built it! At this point of my life, I have had the opportunity to travel, own things, pay off things and gain what I was told I couldn't and wouldn't have. I am no genius and I have mental barriers that sometimes keeps me from pushing through but damn it, I get shit done at the end of the day. I write this to say that you will always have people or circumstances that will doubt your vision or plan for success, but you must stay focused always. However, you must remember that success for one is personal and anything worth having may feel uncomfortable to do, require work and push your limits. You are not your past, disability, situation or others opinion of you, so believe in yourself, make your paths and stay focus because you are capable.

Chapter 4:
Fear

I had always associated fear with the ideas of Jason, Freddy Krueger and Michael Myers. You know the noise at night when you're in the bed and lying in the dark. This type of fear I knew so very well, thanks to the ghost in our house on 8th street. The ghost never tried to scare me to death but made sure a little girl had to cover her head on a cold night, while it sat on my bed when I was asleep and peeked at the TV in the family room. Ok, I know I have lost a few of you but hey, I know what I know. Anyway, as you get older, the fear that takes over becomes so much more disabling and real because it affects our self-esteem and overall wellbeing. In high school, I feared being made a fool by some high school bullies who terrorized my locker for almost 6 months. I missed lunch on some days because I was sitting in front of it hoping to prevent being the lunch rush entertainment. That fear lasted a few months until I found out that my torment was due to a couple stupid and jealous girls that decided to torment me over a boy. So, I'm just going to say a meeting in the hallway one on one when you're supposed to be in class with your whoop that ass outfit on can make people leave you alone. A year later, I started working as a cashier in a very busy hardware store which I would shout out, but they were always pulling me aside because people complained I didn't smile, so no. In this position, I was always fearful about my register count. Every time I counted the register, I would feel my heart beating like crazy, and I didn't need to get fired because I had a phone bill. I had a local land line in my name in my room and it wasn't cheap. How else could I talk to my boyfriend all night? So, you could only be shot 3 times and I had watched a few of my friends be fired for having a bad count and it didn't matter even if it was five cents. They funny thing is, I worked there for almost two years and not for once had a shot slipped! I was afraid out my mind for nothing every week and most likely the reason I had those gray hairs at 18. These fears felt so large at the time but now, I see it was just a small mark on my big picture. Before I became a mother, what I feared most was seeing my relationship end because I was often so invested. I feared dying because so many young people were getting killed or dying from crime and accidents. I thought often about how much I still wanted to do, and so I lived like there was no tomorrow. But for the last 13 years, fears have really stolen a lot of my joy. I fear sometime that I'm not a good mom and provider. I went back to school to obtain a master's degree, but my fear of driving kept my income limited and had stolen opportunities I know I would have been good at. My fear of flying has kept me away from my birth home for over nine years and some vacation spots. When my girls see me, I don't want them to see a stern scary cat. I want them to see a woman with a lot of love and drive that worked on her fears and did the best she could to be a wonder woman. I fear the unknown much more as a mother because I want to protect them from this world of hurt, and at the same time not being soft on them. I fear they don't understand my concerns and see me as this mean mother who demands too much from them. I fear the negative self that comes when things get tough!

When my kids are misbehaving, my husband is not paying attention, the job is not fulfilling, and I am failing at a new idea, I always get depressed and I feel ugly. My fear is depression and the toll it constantly has on my life. However, I am always working on my greatest fear by moving forward with classes, counseling, medication and being around drama free people. Everyone has a specific fear of something that will take control of their lives and prevent them from being all they can be. To be fearful is not a sign of weakness, rather it's an emotion that you tackle repeatedly, but also a sign that you are human.

Chapter 5:
Finance

When it comes to money, I am frugal and cautious about how I spend. I have always been good at stretching a dollar and paying off debt, but I also learned at an early age that the word sale and clearance can be your best friend. My kids will tell you that if it isn't on sale or I don't have a coupon or code to get a discount, I won't buy it and for the most part, that's correct. You see I was not raised wearing labels and I didn't care except on the two occasions that I gave in to it. One of those times was in 8th grade when Keds were the shit and everybody wore them in a variety of colors. I think back then, they were like $25-30 and that was too much for my money, and so I bought the knock off canvas shoes that you could get for $5. Most of the time, I tried to hide the back, so nobody would notice the missing blue label. Well, somebody in the family bought me a pair of Keds when I was in 7th grade for my birthday and when I say I wore them until they could not be washed to even white grey no more, I speak the truth. So, like a few other people I knew, I decide to cut the blue label of the old Keds and add them to my new budget priced shoes with a super glue. For about a week, I was happy, and no one noticed until one day in class while I was looking at the back of my shoe, I noticed the blue label was missing on my right shoe. It was like my entire world stopped and I looked around the room frantically from my seat for the label. What if someone sees my shoes, they would know I couldn't afford Keds and my already mediocre popular status would be ruined, I thought. I was going to die if I didn't find it. After class, I took off running down the hall one to distract people from looking at my shoes and to find my label. Well, guess where it was? It was sitting on the ground in front of my locker! Thank God no one thought to pick it up and throw it away. So, I scooped it up and stuck it back on, but the pride I felt of trying to front was short lived when another student was caught doing the same thing. I sat through a whole class hearing the constant jokes being made about another student who had glued on their label and didn't do such a wonderful job at it. This kid was joked about all day on how poor he was to do that and all other kinds humiliating comments one could ever think of. From that moment, I decided to be me, be my authentic self and I would dare someone to talk trash about me. Of course, that led to some fist fights and curse out sessions, but you knew where things would go if you messed with me. I really started to learn about money around 10 when I could do extra chores in exchange for a brown one-dollar food stamp. Let me tell you, I lived for my mommas lose ones, okay. Back then, you could get kids to clean your whole house for a few brown backs. I'd take one dollar and come back with candy for days. I would be at the corner store making life decisions. I mean I could go with a snickers bar, but it wouldn't last longer than an hour to get a bunch of 1 cent tootsie rolls, a bag of skittles or a 10-cent box of lemon heads, red hots and all other varieties. So, by the time I got my first job at 14 and was making real money, I was almost an expert at bargain shopping. I learned about discount stores like Ross and Marshalls and your off-brand stores like Roses. I didn't like spending my hard-earned money on school cloths and supplies, but dang it I made it happen even with $300. I was going to be fly the first day at school. Having a large family also allowed me to learn the skill of one pot meals and nobody was better than finding 3-4 ingredients to make a meal with. She would be like, "well, we have a bag of noodles, a can of mixed vegetables, four drumsticks and some top roman noodles sauce packets in the cabinet." I used to say I hate those made-up soups, but now I find myself making soup for my family. My point is, I learned to value a dollar and I learned to have something to show for it. I understand that brands mean something to some people because it shows your elevation or superficial status. I get it and I'm not mad at you if you really can afford it. However, you should always save some money for a rainy day and I don't care if it's two dollars a check. If buying the latest in name brands doesn't allow that, then you're doing things wrong. Take care of your necessities first and let me repeat that again "Your necessities first!" Things like your rent, utilities and food are necessities not your cable, car note, hair style, nails and whatever else you don't need to live life. If you can only afford a studio, don't get a two-bedroom apartment and if you can't afford a house move in an apartment. I see so many people trying to be like other people by checking their pockets and oftentimes, they have no idea what that person is doing to get by. If it's a want, don't get it unless you have extra money to buy it. I am going to give you some money insight that works for my family, which my husband hates, it but it works. So, let's say you have been wanting to get a new television, you know the one with all the bells and whistles, that will cover the whole wall in the family room and you must sit in the kitchen just to enjoy it. Yeah, that TV is going to cost you $1200. Now, once you're done paying your necessities, and you have $200 and a credit card with a balance of $1400 and a limit of $5k. I know a lot of people who will go and purchase this TV today, but a smart money person would consider the following. First, the TV is hot right now but by this time next year it won't be as hot as it is now. Second, I would get the TV, but it would come from one of two places; my credit card or my taxes. It depends on how much I get each year. If I receive around $1k monthly, I would just buy the TV straight up because in a year it would have gone down by $200, but if I am building my credit, I would use the tax money on my credit card and buy the TV with it. I would never increase the balance or get a new card unless I got some percentage off for a new account and then I would pay that bill in full and close the account. Third, you may have to watch your out-of-date set for another year but Rent-a- Center can't pick up your stuff because of missed payment and you're still on track with your bills. I also choose to live and spend like I have never gotten a raise, which means trying to live on one person's salary if possible and using the rest for emergency and wants. I see so many couples go out and buy a home with a mortgage of $1500-$1700 a month, and as soon as one of them loses a job, they face foreclosure! Live off a third of your income if possible; get a reliable car with an extra warranty and plan on having it for at least ten years. Shop in bulk for dry goods and check out your local 2nd hand stores and you will be surprised what jewels you will find. I know it's not everyone's cup of tea to brag or post on FB about what a great deal they got on a clearance rack with a coupon, but hey, I got some nice deals. If I can put together a whole outfit for under $30, I feel very accomplished. Now on to a real important note concerning finance, it is very beneficial to have a life insurance policy and best to get a term of 10-30 years or more because so many people die, and their families get stuck with bills and taking money from their savings for a loved one's going home celebration. I know most don't want to face this fact, but real talk is important. Last and not the least, put some money aside for retirement unless you plan on working until your last breath. I mean everyone deserves to sit on the porch with a stiff drink and a smoke and talk trash as many days as they like.

Chapter 6:
Freaking

The first thing I will say about this is if you are under 19 and are seriously engaging in the wonderful world of sex, you don't know shit! I don't care if you have been having sex since you were 13. The act of intimacy has so many layers, which can take time for you to understand them, what you need and desire for your pleasure. Most of us didn't have the sex education talk with our parents while we were still growing up as kids, and we often just go out and experiment on our own. Our parents focus more on pregnancy and school, and at the same time they scare you with STD photos. So, getting through high school without a baby or disease is your goal, but really understanding the truth about sex and what it brings to your life usually isn't realized until years later. If you have been capable of not getting pregnant outside marital life, you are either lucky as hell or you could be using the proper precautionary measures, but most of you don't really depend on the sex class at school to teach you about all the diseases out there and the emotional toll it takes on your mind and body once you jump into this world sex. Sex is often so taboo, and parents don't care to talk about it much until it's too late. We are always telling our kids not to do it and still threaten them with consequences if we find out any irrational behavior. Now in no way am I saying you should turn your house into the hoe hum, but I think that a clear and no filtered conversation is important for parents and teens. I started being active at the age of 17, and that was toward the end of my junior year. My focus was always on not getting pregnant and I had been dating the same boy for a while, and so I felt like I was in love with him. Two years earlier I offered a boy some cookies because I wanted to show him I was loyal, but my childish expression was met with a no because he knew I wasn't ready. I had no idea how much sex changes you, both in a positive and negative way. The best part of sex for me has been the feeling of attraction and affection. Most of us feel beautiful, but there is something different about someone saying I really find you beautiful. I often felt un-pretty, and as I got older this attention contradicted that feeling that has taken a bigger part of me. Along with this, I became confidant and secured in my looks so much so that at the age of 19, I got a tattoo on my left arm that boldly read sexy. Yes, I had a lot of women hating on me for getting that, but on the other hand the guys loved my confidence. I slowly confused love for lust and with that I lost myself. I didn't grow up with a father telling me that I am pretty or important, and so I had no real expectation or example of what love truly looked like. Eventually, I deeply felt love for men who only saw me as a play girl and afterwards came heartache. After that I learned there was a difference between love and sex. I never had to make the difficult decision of having a baby, or even getting an abortion, and this was achieved only by the grace of God. As an unplanned child, I was very vigilant on staying protected from that kind of event, but I witnessed often that this has being a question for others. What a difficult decision to face because of the joy of sex. It was the right decision for some and a lifelong regret for others. I also saw the less talked about the effects of sex and the diseases that can practically take over your life and end it in the process. There is so much shit that was skipped out there in school! When our hormones get to raging, you start feeling grown. When really, we are just starting to understand our own bodies likes and dislikes. We hate to follow the words and advice of our elders because we feel we know it all. Sometimes, you gain unwanted attention and most times that leads to rape and molestation both for boys and girls. If you ever feel threatened or have been violated, please share the experience with someone else. Don't allow the person or people to continue violating you, because you didn't ask or deserve their abuse. I personally love sex as it's almost like a drug in some ways to me. It makes you feel much better almost all the time no matter the situation, and like drugs only for a limited time! Sex also comes with a page of shame when a little bit of fun turns into a ball of stigma or a fight for your life. No one is looking to catch something from another person on purpose, but unfortunately our world is not made for people to be honest about their status, even when it comes to those friends or family you are not sleeping with. The lack of knowledge, information and the belief that we already know about puts everyone who is sexually active at risk. Deciding to be sexually active may not always bring you the joy you were looking for, and this is the hard lesson we all learn over time. Now, I don't want to have sex to seem like a shameful act, disgusting and hurtful, but rather just something to think about when deciding to do the humpty hump. So, with all the doom and gloom out of the way let's swerve to the fun honest stuff! Well, I'm going to start with the ladies because I am a lady in the daytime. Now, men are not all big perverts that are waiting to pounce as soon as you take your drawers off, they also need some attention too. So, what I am saying is if you are a lay there please me type of chick, please check your game before a can't stop and won't stop freak roll up on you. If your man likes oral pleasure and that isn't really your thing, don't expect it to last or not have him step out because men always complain. They share just like we ladies do, then when some other chick that loves to do that freak thing is going to roll up on him. If your man met you thick and soft then you are alright physically, but if you turn soft and extra thick and he has not said anything, it's not always because he loves the looks, but because he loves you, don't get confused about the two. If you don't compliment your man and tell him that he's looking fine, squeeze his butt and slide your hand over his manhood occasionally, some thirsty freak is going to roll up looking to drink all his cool aid. Men, this goes for you too! Don't under estimate her love or your bedroom boot knocking sessions as a reason for her to staying with you. A woman needs just as much and if not more recognition and validation from her man. Why? Well, it's most likely that she is working fulltime. So, she is making the money to buy the bacon, buying the bacon, cooking the bacon for everyone in the house and then cleaning that greasy kitchen. Women are out there doing various jobs that had only belonged to our men for a long time. I think we have forgotten the fact that we are women, we need to be told that we are appreciated, that we are beautiful and that you still get hard when you see use walk by a little bit of nothing. We often forget what we have at home and we focus on the things that our partner does that gets on our last nerve. My husband and I are as guilty as any couple when it comes to this, and it has really put some hurting on our relationship. In the beginning of our relationship we were hot and sexy ready for love all night long! Now I want to keep up with the young me, but my knee is like girl please and my back is saying what the hell are you thinking?! I can't fit into my size 8 panties anymore and I had to move up to a sexy woman's 14, but hey I recognized that my man still needs attention so if it means that I will be in a knee brace and taking extra strength Motrin to put on a circus act night, I am down and I want the same in return. As people, we are always learning new ideas and taking on new perspectives, so why would our sex lives be any different? Our desires and how it's delivered may change and if so, hopefully you have a mate that you can be open and honest with. You should be your truest self with the one you share your bed with because you are at your most vulnerable mentally and physically with this person. If you must keep things to yourself or hide your desires for something, you only push yourself away from your mate more and more. Eventually, leading to no sex or cheating on your partner.

Chapter 7:
Fitness

I can remember a time when I could eat whatever I wanted! I can remember being in 12th grade and eating chocolate cake everyday so that I could get thick because my boyfriend likes a girl on the curvy side. I was born with the dumps in the truck, but no lights on the grill, so I thought eating would fill me out all over. I could stay around 130 pounds until I reached 28, and then my weight started to fluctuate between 140-145 lbs. and at 5'3' I became overweight. So, I placed myself on diet to get a few pounds off every year. I hit my highest weight of 212 lbs. when I was 36. I still didn't think I looked fat, until one day I stood in front of a floor to a ceiling mirror in my hotel room. I looked like a bag of cottage cheese with dimples and stretchmarks from my navel downwards. I was disgusted and when I turned around to see 4-6 back rolls, I thought where the hell have I been that I didn't notice my body had turned into the Pillsbury Dough boys mother! I remember lying in the bed next to my husband thinking that I will never let anyone see me naked again and how could he stand to touch me. When I got home, I ordered my Hip Hop Abs workout tap and Sean T became my best friend for about two months. I started off with my daughter as my partner, but she wasn't committed enough to stay on the run with me. The first day, I almost had a heart attack trying to keep up with my boy toy Mr. T. I was sweating like a drop of water in hot pan, I was a mess. I started with the Atkins Diet again because up to this point it was the only thing that had really worked for me. I have tried almost everything from the grapefruit, cabbage diets to the lemon, cayenne pepper and honey drink. I was open to losing weight and willing to try almost anything. By the time, I finished the program twice in a row, I went on to Insanity and yes that is a correct name for what Sean wants you to do. But you know what? I was 20lbs smaller and feeling sexier than ever. I still had cottage cheese but less of it, and my stomach had gone down and my dresses were also hitting my curves rightly! I was almost about to throw the Spanx out because I didn't have the rolls popping out of my cloths anymore. I had more stamina in the bedroom and my body didn't need any Motrin from me trying to show off. I still wasn't my desired weight, but I felt great until I had a tragedy that came and stole my joy. Now some people are emotional eaters and up to this point, I didn't realize that this was something I did. My close friend passed away suddenly only a few hours after I had left her home. I was so pissed, hurt and lonely because she had been many things in my life for the past 8 years and in a flash, she was gone. I didn't really notice how I started to drop workout sessions or how my diet was failing. I just wanted to see my friend again and stressed over how lonely I had become. Then one day I looked in the mirror again and I was 212 pounds and back to the old disgusted me. My doctors noticed the weight gain as well and suggested that I lose a large amount of weight. I really felt like I didn't know how because I was 40 with less motivation and still carried around a bag full of new stressors. I wanted to feel the energy and confidence again, but my cravings were stronger than my will to look great. I went to get a boob job thinking it would motivate me to become a hot momma. I gave my butt something to even me out, but I still had the morning knee pain and granny walk after sitting in a chair for too long. After having another baby in 2012, I told myself that I really wanted to be around for her, but my focus didn't have enough action to make any desirable change that I wished for. I have invested in exercise videos, trainer, home gym and a gym membership so I have no good reason to still be hefty, hefty, hefty! So, for anyone that is struggling I can understand the battle between fat and fit. Being physically fit is not just for the vain or because you're afraid to be body shamed. We all should not hesitate to be at our best capable health status. When I say be fit I don't mean be skinny or sculpted with a 6 pack. I mean the type of fit that allows you to have energy, strength, control of your insulin and cholesterol levels. I personally want to be able to walk around my neighborhood without breathing hard or needing ice for my body. I just want to make it clear that curvy is still sexy. So, I am not promoting losing all the fat. I just want to set a good example of making a difference by taking on the challenge to living a healthier and happier life. I am my children's first role model and I accept that responsibility wholeheartedly.

Chapter 8:
Frustration

At times, I get so mad and my heart would sound like a tribe preparing for war. In my head, there are three of us hitting on a bass drum with baseball bats, and NaNa is leading the way. I have been working on my desire to lay my hands, fist and other weapons on people after being disrespected or treated unfairly. I regularly visit an anger management group every Friday and have done so for the last two years because I am still working on it. I personally choose to call my anger frustration, because it comes from a place of love and there was a need to have someone leave me the hell alone. There have only been a few times I may have ended up in jail, in solitary and butt naked with a loaf meal. One of those almost moments was when I had a hair appointment and I had taken my vacation time to go. I tried my best to get a Saturday appointment, but after looking at my schedule and the Beauticians schedule, I had to settle for a Wednesday appointment. So, since I knew my 2:30 appointment would last until 8pm, I had to also find a sitter for my daughter. So, on this beautiful Tuesday afternoon I left work and drove 20 minutes pass the salon to get my daughter from daycare. I took her to the sitter's house, I then drove to the hair store and bought 2 packs of 12" yucky straight 1B/27. Now I can't remember the brand, but most likely it was on sale and it was not the best hair and I still asked for a discount. Anyways, I sat in the car outside the shop for about 10 minutes looking at photos of how I wanted my new style to look once she hooked me up. So, at exactly 2:30, I went up to the door and tried to open it then I found out that it was locked. If you know me, you will know that I am late to everything. So, to make it there on time meant I was ready for her to do her thang and make me cute before I left the shop. Well, my first thought is maybe she stepped out to get a meal and then I went back to the car. I sat for 1hour and no one showed up! I then called the shop and left a message on the phone thinking that maybe she thought I didn't show up. I continued to sit in my car another 45 minutes after leaving the message. So, when I felt my patience had had enough, this trifling heifer came rolling up in her car and parked a few cars down from mine. She got out, looked dead at me and started to walk toward the door of the shop. I got out of my car and said, "Hey I have been waiting on you for almost two hours, you could have called me and had me come later." She turned around and started to walk toward me and I mean all 5'4 250-280lbs of her and said when she got to me "I don't have time to do your hair today, you have to come back another time!" She then turned around and started walking her big ass back toward the stairwell. All I could think in that moment was "This fat ugly B got me all mixed up if she thinks this is alright with me. I took 3.5 hours off work, drove 40 minutes out of the way, paid a sitter $40 dollars and waited for almost 2 hours for her to say she doesn't have time!" However, what I said was "Well I had to take time off and get a sitter for this appointment. If you would have called me I wouldn't have taken the time off." It was obvious she wanted to fight and to be honest, I wanted to beat this B's ass for trying me, because she turned back around and started walking back and told me to "Reschedule since she wouldn't do it today." By this time, I was plotting my beat down method step by step because I was detailed like that. Well, while my right hand was preparing to give her the first blow under the chin, my left hand happens to grab my lanyard with my work ID on it, and I realized that I was an adult with a child. My husband was overseas, so if I decided to act a straight fool with this chick and give her what she was asking for, who would take care of my child? I had to decide that my pride wasn't worth putting my foot on her neck and going to jail. As she got closer, I felt my eyes getting watery, because I had to decide on letting her know that I don't play when it comes to my time and money or let her think she just punked me! I chose my daughter and asked her "What's wrong?" When she got closer, she said "I had to get my daughter. I don't have time for this so reschedule if you want it done". Now, I had to hold on to my lanyard the whole time to keep me in check, because this time when she came to me her daughter, who was around 17 was with her, and she was standing there looking like she wanted me to add her to the ass whooping list. My mind had not added her yet, so I was not prepared for that episode. Instead, I got into my car and cried all the way home calling her every insult and bad word I could think of. To be honest, I think insulted her in my mind for a whole week and a little right now as I am write about the incident. I guess my point is if you don't have a baby get one, and if you don't have a job get one, or something else that is extremely important to you so could you have a few things to keep your grown ass from going to jail! Being or becoming frustrated with yourself, others and situations will happen repeatedly and guess what, it is also a lesson to be learned each time as well. I am learning all the time about myself and what have become my new priorities. I am learning what must be a battle and how to forgive myself. I am learning that tears and silence don't mean weakness because it takes a lot of strength for the strong to stay silent. Mostly, I have learned to lead with my mind and heart because I need them to check on each other always. Also, a little tip I use are photos. I have them in my car, desk and as screen savers on my phone. I need to be reminded sometime while I am staying silent.

Chapter 9:
Faith

I could have written a book just about faith because I have seen the power of prayer repeatedly! I was raised in the church and I would say I am a strong believer and a follower of Jesus Christ and the almighty God. However, I am not religious, but like most people I am good at using the word to fit my beliefs toward others behavior, and as a lose guideline for my life. These types of people are often called hypocrites, and I would be lying if I said I didn't fall in this category at times. I think the biggest issue I have with religion is religious people, because they are so full of judgement, but only toward others. The funny thing is we judge based on where people are, and not where they are trying to go. I have been blessed so much and abundantly by God and I would like to think I deserve it, but if God judged us by his laws I would have been long condemned to a life with no grace or mercy. So, I found out that I am willing to forgive those who have hurt me, apologize when I don't feel wrong to bring peace and try to understand that my journey is not the journey for everyone. I believe that if I love others with a true heart, and in the way that the lord has intended, things will work out just fine. They may not work out to my understanding or desire at the time, but eventually things always seemed to make sense in the long run. I am going to share a few stories that I have no doubt are true blessing from the Lord. I didn't receive these blessings because I am a better Christian, because I paid more money in tithes or because I am without sin. I just stopped trying to control every aspect my life. I had to see and believe my prayers were being heard by God. As I prayed, my spirit moved to desires I had not had before and toward actions that seemed to pull me away from my desired results. The birth of my children came with some sadness, jealousy and great fear. With each pregnancy, I had bed rest, gestational diabetes, concerns with hearing a steady heartbeat and gallons of tears praying that God would heal my body and so I bear children within my marriage. My children are eight years apart, but each took around four years of constant doctor's appointments and drugs to conceive. Many times, I felt I was being punished for supporting others, and even sometimes encouraging them to end their pregnancies in abortions. My mother and many others told me that God didn't treat his children this way. So, I had to believe that the Lord knew my heart then as well as now and just trust the process in which God would work in my life. Now, 13 years later I saw my desire and troubles with conceiving as a well sought out plan for my life. It allowed me to know myself and the lengths I would go to for something I really wanted. I appreciated the distance between my children because it allowed me the time to focus on each child per their needs. God gave my husband and I time to work on our marriage and put us in a financial situation that would allow my children a chance to get to see and know their grandmothers. I see more now than I ever thought could be true for me. I took my pain as God's example of letting me know he didn't love me, and that I was a disappointment, instead of understanding that all that seemed good is not always good at that time. I often think about my children that didn't make it. I wonder how they would have looked and if they may have been boys. I miss them to this day because they lived in me and each time I hug my daughters, I thank God for his precious gift in my life. I believe in God and Jesus Christ, not just because I was told too, but because I have witnessed situations whereby it was only by God that things worked out. Some may call it coincidence, but I call it the spirit and the angels of heaven who have brought me through some sticky situations. I know one day a situation will take me home and for some it will seem unfair, too soon or even tragic, but I understand that my life has been filled with a lot of grace and mercy that allowed me the chance to do so many of my heart's desires.

Chapter 10:
Finally

What will others say about you once you're dead and gone? Hopefully, they will share how your life inspired and changed them for the better. At least, I hope that is what people share about me. I was born with the understanding that you live only to die. This thinking puts a frantic feeling in me every time I participated in something I wasn't sure of. I was afraid of elevators, escalators, ladders, dogs and the slimy skin on chicken wings! Yes, the skin on chicken wings had to be crunchy, and if it wasn't, I would just try to swallow it because I hated the way it tastes. Have you ever had a piece of chicken skin stuck in your throat because it didn't go way down, yeah it is scary trying to cough it out. I had to stop doing that because I didn't want that to be the reason to die. I couldn't imagine a scenario with people coming up to my mom saying what happened and she is replying with tears in her eyes "She choked on chicken skin." Yeah, not me! I know that many people have different religions or relationships when it comes to God. I was raised as a Christian and non-denominational. I have held on too many of my beliefs from childhood. At times, I question things I have learned or actions that caused great grief in the hearts of those who believe. At times, I thought to abandon my faith but time after time, I felt convicted and returned. I have found believing in the son of God, Jesus Christ, and the chance of living in eternity with all your needs meet in a love filled heaven, which allows my heart a chance to heal when a close friend or family members passes on. I choose to believe that I will one day see those who meant so much to me during my life. In the moment, when I fear the end, I feel the joy of those loved ones saying welcome home. Now, I am sure some people are not on board with the idea of heaven and hell, but it gives me hope and strength. For me anything that empowers me to do Good among my brothers and sisters in Christ, I'm for it because there are a lot of factors that make you want to give up. I have lost some friends and a hand full of family members, but my hardest moments dealing with death had to be when I had multiple miscarriages and when my friend, Velma, passed. Until this day, I wonder who my twins would have looked like and their sex. But I also take pleasure in thinking they will greet me when I pass, and I will recognize them right away. My best friend, Velma, was almost 30 years my senior but she felt maybe it was 10. She was a mother/sister to me and a grandmother to my oldest child. I learned how to cook from scratch and ignored the small stuff with her at my side. She supported every vision I had for myself and was my constant cheerleader. Like most people, we disagreed but never had anything that caused us not to talk longer than two days. We spent holiday's together, swapped recipes and went to do my favorite thing in the world, wig shopping! I loved her like family and when she died, it was obvious all my family felt that way about her too. I know this chapter was about death, but I can't talk about death without bringing up my Lord and Savior, Jesus Christ. You see, I believe He knew how much I loved Velma and He allowed me the chance to see her on the day she passed. I spent almost two hours with her before she passed. We talked about almost every subject on the planet in that little bit of time. I left that day telling her I appreciated her friendship and hugging her. Unaware that we would never speak again, I felt I shared all I needed to share with her that day. I was called within thirty minutes of her passing away and when I rushed to her home, she was still there. I had the opportunity to touch her and fix her up a little, but at that moment, I also thanked God for the opportunity to spend time with her that morning. I still feel hurt at times when I want to call and throw my ideas at her, but I can't. I do take pride in knowing she believed in me, and so I kept pressing. Now in my life, I want to mend relationships and get rid of old wounds. I want to speak only positivity to others and in my life. I don't want to regret not saying I love you, before a loved one walks out the door. I appreciate the moments I have with my children more because I see how fast life is moving around me. Most of all, I think about how I treat people and what will be said to my children about me once I am gone. I want my children to know I was hard, but soft at the same time. I try continuously to prepare them for what the world is going to throw at them in my absence. Hopefully, 'What the F' will serve as a voice for my children to challenge people, places or things that make them feel less than who they are. Most especially, I want to make it possible for them to be confident in who they are and who they will become. I also want to allow them look at their obstacles, achievements and desires as lessons to see them thru life.

Extra:

Now I like to consider myself a life guru but I can't even lie. I am aware that my experiences only cover some of the lessons that need to be learned or shared. So, I reached out to family, friends and social media to see if they had anything to share about things they have learned throughout their lives. Most people wanted to share quotes but a few had some short stories that will make you appreciate the sunshine after the rain. I hope you find confirmation, peace and comradery in the words of those who transparently shared with us.

Family

"Everyone needs love but many can't show it because it is a sign of weakness for them. It is hard to be venerable because you risk being taken advantage of and that hurts more than pretending not to care." **Nameless**

"I'm at a point in my life where I want to get to know my family members that I have not known and those I have not seen in a long time. I want to fill this void of those I never met by meeting them someday and hugging them. I would say to people to get to know your family and realize how big it is." **Antonio McKinney**

"When your parents can trust you to be honest in your actions when you're with or without them your childhood allows so many more experiences." **Nameless**

"If your sibling is going through something and they decide to share it with you realize that sometimes you have to accept that you may not be needed to fix it but instead an arm to lean on and a listening ear." **Nameless**

"Teenagers attitudes…Don't ever take anything personal." **Karen Massey**

"I live in my moment a lot because I choose to deal with my pain or joy so that I can experience what's next. Staying in the past takes away so much of your future so learn to forgive." **Nameless**

"It's hard to explain the feeling of love but once it hits you boy can you recognize it. Sometimes it may come at a time you are not looking for it or you feel it for someone who is obviously all wrong for you. Its power can save many lives or take them away and I truly believe no other emotion is greater." **Nameless**

"Most likely you are doing something that will last with your child forever." **Nameless**

I wish I could baby my child forever and give them their every desire but the real world doesn't feel the same." **Nameless**

"I use to hate the lecture from my mom before and after a whopping but I can say I never thought I didn't do anything to deserve it or she did it because she didn't love me." **Nameless**

"A little bit of get right teaches actions and consequences." **Nameless**

"The idea of structure scares some people but if more children had structure we wouldn't see so much disrespect for authority and the elderly."

Family "my first child was single parented by me, and it was HARD. I never cease to be amaze how much easier life is when you have family to love and support you. Family isn't always blood, and support is sometimes just them having faith in you." **Kelly Schenkman**

Family "What I've learned is that no matter what you go through family will be there for you. Whether they are friends you come to call family or blood relatives. And it's ok to let go of those in your life that mean you harm." **Robyn Byrd**

"Hopefully ratchet television and video games are not the teachers of upright moral practice in your home because our children are looking for role models." **Nameless**

"It can be so hard trying to love people where there are especially when they don't realize how it hurts you. It's alright to love from a far until there has been a change in you or them." **Nameless**

"Blood is thicker than water but if you dilute it with anything it isn't any good same thing with those family members who don't give anything positive. "**Nameless**

"I didn't get to have all four of my grandparents around that much but I did know who they were and I learned a little about each of them from our brief encounters. However, my maternal grandfather always made me feel beautiful and smart. He was the first man who made me feel I was somebody and could do whatever I dreamed of and for that I think of him every time I want to give up." **Natasha Knight**

Friends----
"I believe your vibe attracts your tribe. Be such a positive light that those who have dark intentions will want to either come over to the light and join you or stay away. Don't let anyone dim that light and keep on shining." **Jennifer Durham**

"I feel that there is only a few people that remain in your life as a friend for the long haul. Everyone has a season in your life rather it be short term or long term. I cherish every friendship that I have ever had because however long they were around I learned something from them rather good, bad, or in between. A good loyal friend is hard to find but when you find them hold on to them. Don't take them for granted because they are Truly hard to find truly a blessing." **Tynesha Bright**

"There are some people that are quick to pass judgement based on one moment in your life they may be privileged to see. And begin to make assumptions on who you are and how you live. I saw a saying on Facebook, and it said don't judge my book by the chapter you walked in on. Instead be a friend and support them so don't add a chapter to their book that changes the outcome of their story." **Esther McInnis**

"A person whom has an undying mutual relationship with respect that does not judge you nor tries to change you but instead tries to understand you." **L. Bishop**

"If we have great conversation and are there for each other in times of need. If she/he cares about my overall well-being." **Aisha Mitchell**

Focus

"If you take the good things from your childhood and build your life upon those things and take the bad as things as lessons you will be surprised by how much you can accomplish." **Nameless**

"In Life, there will be challenges and obstacles but if you wake up every morning there's time for change." **Marshea Boyd**

"we seem to think in terms of, "When I..." as though this imagined destination will make our lives complete. More than a specific accomplishment, we are supposed to enjoy the journey. Every part of it is about us being shaped, and not the other way around. Nothing wrong with focus, but as my mentor says, "you're seeing the right thing, but are you seeing it, right?" **Mercedes Munoz**

Finance

"I live by the motto that every dollar has a name. I try to budget for every possible spend and label it so. Just like planning to eat. I plan what I spend." **Melissa McClary Davis**

"Start saving...it's never too late. Enroll in a 401K and a Roth IRA." **Jamarsae Brown Sr.**

"Do not let your love for finance overshadow your family it's definitely needed to live comfortable but one can never buy back the time that has been lost with your family immediate or extended so value it because that family time is precious we never know wat tomorrow may bring." **Dontae Massey**

Fear

"I have learned that Fear can grip you and make you stop living life. But it's an emotion that you can experience and let go so you can face the challenge presented to you. I was diagnosed with Blood Cancer and for a whole year, I was frozen in fear. But now that I have faced death, I am more interested in life and learning to enjoy it and learning how to treat myself, what works for me and makes me feel better." **Laurel Hughes**

"False…Expectations…Appearing...Real until you decide to Face…Everything…And... Rise!!!" **Agnes Arletha Neal**

"fear is a normal emotion. However, it becomes abnormal when you use it as an excuse or let it stand in the way of your dreams!!!" **Claudette Beulah Pettyjohn**

"It seems as though we do everything with an undertone of fear. Which makes sense, since it is a prime instinct for survival. I've learned to trust my instincts. Not to second Guess so much. I can say that through doing so, I have been able to be there for my kids and other people based on our close connections." **Lisa A F Mughal**

Freaking

"If you single and mingle, don't date anyone around your home and at your job. Put yourself first. If you are involved/married and your partner mess with someone at your or a family member… don't waste no time hitting the exit." **Larrysha Ahart-upshaw**

"What looks good to you might not be good for you." **Jamarsae Brown Sr.**

"Sex is the best feeling in the world especially when the one you're with turns on all your scenes." **Nameless**

"Don't be afraid to try something new or different, you miss out on a lot of things being so closed minded." **Nameless**

"Learn how to please yourself, explore your own body." **Nameless**

"Don't be afraid to ask your partner to use protection." **Nameless**

"Sharing your body with someone doesn't make them love you, it just leaves you screwed." **Nameless**

"No sticky in the bottom." **Nameless**

"Be open to trying what your partner wants at least once." **Nameless**

"Never Stop until you get a nut." **Nameless**

"Don't be scared to live a little." **Nameless**

"Don't send naked pictures or make videos." **Nameless**

Faith- "There's going to be some rain most of you know who I am, but not all of you know who's I am. I am not just Renae from Portland, mother of Naomi, wife of Robert. I am a child of the King and a walking miracle who has been chosen to give him the glory. I had symptoms for many years that doctors passed off as migraines or hormonal during my pregnancy. But right after Naomi was born, I was diagnosed with a giant congenital aneurysm (the size of a red potato) in my right temporal lobe. My neurosurgeons did the operation (November 7, 2003) to insert a clip on my carotid artery at the sight of the defect to slowly correct the problem. I came out

of that surgery fine and quoting the 27th Psalm & singing "In my life Lord be glorified". But the next day (November 8, 2003), I took a turn for the worst. Because of the size of the aneurysm, I had a massive bleed that caused my brain to hemorrhage, and was at the point of death. Doctors told my husband and family (who had all flown in from Portland) that they were sorry but they feared I was as good as dead. As a last resort, my neurosurgeons did another surgery to try and relieve the bleeding and save my life. They told my family that they weren't sure if it would work but that it was up to God. And Praise God look at me now! I have some battle scars but I will not complain because I am still here and God has been glorified in my life! I can now look back and see God's favor and how he has had a calling on my life from the beginning. His perfect will and plan for me was already in the making. After having come to Raleigh 10 years ago, on exchange from OSU to NCSU for one year, I found myself at home in Portland feeling as though God was leading me back to Raleigh. I didn't know why then I had to move 3000 miles away. I just knew that I was meant to be here. After moving back, I met my wonderful husband. I am so grateful to have him. We had been married only 2 years when all this happened. Robert took off 2 months of work so that he could be there to help me get well and aid my mother in taking care of our precious baby girl. Not an evening went by in the month that I was in the hospital that he did not bring Naomi to see me. He also came to the hospital every morning to go to therapy with me. Whenever I was losing my will to fight, God placed an encouraging word on his lips to help me go on and reach my goal of getting my left side strong enough to learn how to walk again. When I got out of the hospital and my mother left and Robert went back to work, he took Naomi and I with him whenever he had to go out of town until I felt able to take care of her on my own. Did I say how wonderful Robert is!? I am so blessed to have my little angel Naomi, who is no doubt God sent. She came 2 weeks early, which was exactly 2 weeks before doctors found this time bomb in my head. This didn't just happen by chance! Because of God working through her, I am here. God also gave me my doctors, the world-renowned Dr. Takanori Fukushima & Dr. Russell Margraf, who fit me in to their schedule at the last minute and took on my case when other doctors were unwilling to operate on the largest un-ruptured brain aneurysm ever found in the history of Duke Hospital records. I am so very thankful to all my family, friends and everyone that God placed in my life to be instrumental in my healing process. They have done so much for me. Where would I be and what would I have done without them? Everything has worked out for my good and for his glory. How do I know that God has been glorified? Well...from hearing my niece (who at the time was only 4) say "T'Nae, I remember when you were sick in the hospital and almost died, but Jesus, he saved you!", to my husband's co-worker (who was somewhat an atheist) tell me "Renae, I truly have seen the goodness of the Lord in your life!". These are just some of the affirmations that God was using me. They helped me realize the purpose in my storm. So now when rain comes, I am not fearful. I know that it's just a season and that God is doing a great work in me so that he will get the glory and that I will be stronger & ready for my harvest and the work that he has for me to do. I am just so honored that he appointed me for the task. If I was asked to do it all again, I would with no question. Even though I had to suffer, it all makes sense now. All of this was a part of God's perfect plan for me. Now that the storm is over, I can see clearly now and look back at everything that happened and say "Oh, that's why you allowed that to happen Lord!". I once heard someone say "If I had never been sick Lord, how would I have known you were my healer?" This holds so true to my life. I just think of myself as a flower now. And I look at the rain as a part of growing. I repeat the words in my mind sung by my all-time favorite group Commissioned "If there had not been any rain, how would I ever grow?" My intention of sharing my story is not to tell everyone how hard my plight has been, but to show them what my God can do and to encourage some one that may be in a rainy season to keep the faith and hold on to the promises of God until the storm is over." **O Renae Cain English**

"I find myself constantly in conflict when it comes to the word of God. I know what It says but I find myself having so many questions and doubts because the book was interpreted by man. I have never met a man I can trust." **Nameless**

"Faith to me has meant to believe something further than what you have been through, where you come from, what you use to be and beyond what you can imagine. It was something i had when i didn't have money, a friend, when i wanted to throw in the towel, when situations were beyond my control, when i didn't have the right answer and more. Jesus says that he can't be pleased without. For the word says without faith it is impossible to believe God. I confessed a prayer and through grace and by faith my life has changed." **Collena Hope**

"It is very powerful! Complete trust in God is a must. It is not always easy but it is necessary. When you strive to reach complete trust in god you will have a peace that passes all understanding! People will wonder how you made it through difficult times in your life and still seem to be okay and it will be because you have strong faith. Knowing everything happens for a reason and that all things come together for the good for those that love God is Powerful!" **Arielle Jordan**

"I know without a doubt if it wasn't for God's grace and mercy I wouldn't be here. I will forever give him the praise for all that he's done in my life. I thank God has taught to love all my people. #forevergrateful." **Bridgette Brown**

"God is still writing your story, don't let go of your faith because of what you have yet to see." **Nickcolynn Nixon**

"After my ex of 25 years asked me for a divorce it was nobody but God and His word that got me through. The Lord loved me more than I loved myself and that's why God gave His only begotten son to die for us on the cross so that we can repent and be born again. Therefore, after much prayer the Lord restored my peace and strength to get through the devastation that I endured. And, I could forgive my ex because in the word it states "He (the Lord) will not forgive us of our trespasses unless we forgive others". Therefore, I didn't want the Lord to take His hands off me and for me not to be covered under His will." **Melanie Richardson-Phillips**

Fitness

"#NoExcuses." **Eric Forte'**

"Keep pushing & be healthy my friends." **Collin A. Jackson**

"Stay motivated! Be disciplined and ignore the haters!" **Deonte Hall**

"Hard work beats talent, when talent don't work hard." **Gerard Carry**

"Health is wealth." **Lawrence Hairston**

"I always tell myself if it was easy everybody would be doing it." **Lenez Sanders**

"It's necessary and essential." **Brendan Brown**

Frustration

"Stress. Don't let it control you, you control it. Bad stress has a way of sneaking into our lives and taking over but we must be stronger than it is. It will have you thinking different, acting different, and looking different because what we let bother us on the inside will show on the outside. At one point, I started sweating the small stuff until I finally got tired of worrying about things I had no control over it. If it's a person that is stressing you out, don't ask god to change then ask him to change you. When I did, I realized he didn't change me as a person but my way of thinking. Once my way of thinking changed, everything was much better. I felt better, I slept better, I laughed better, heck, I even cried better. Don't let it hold you down and smother the life out of you. Remember that stress comes from our thoughts of our own situations. We can't escape it but we can decide what we want to do with it. Being stressed out is very serious." **Kimmery Merriman**

"It's only just a season. Chances are that in the next 5 hours/days i won't remember what i was so frustrated about. Keeping this in mind has greatly reduced my reaction to frustrating incidences". **Kay Anyachor**

"Be easy on yourself and forgive yourself. We all have too much to do and we can allow ourselves to accept that sometimes, I suck and it's okay." **Gina Nobile**

"God gave us our brains so we could work out problems, however, sometimes we use it to add more problems to our plate by overthinking and/or harboring feelings. Stress is a killer. Talk about how you're feeling. Never ignore it!" **Nameless**

Finally

"I just know the recovery time is brutal for those left behind." **Tara Stevens**

"Death scares me, yet I think about it often." **Natasha Knight**

"Sometimes you don't realize how much you love someone until you can't touch, talk or laugh with them again." **Nameless**